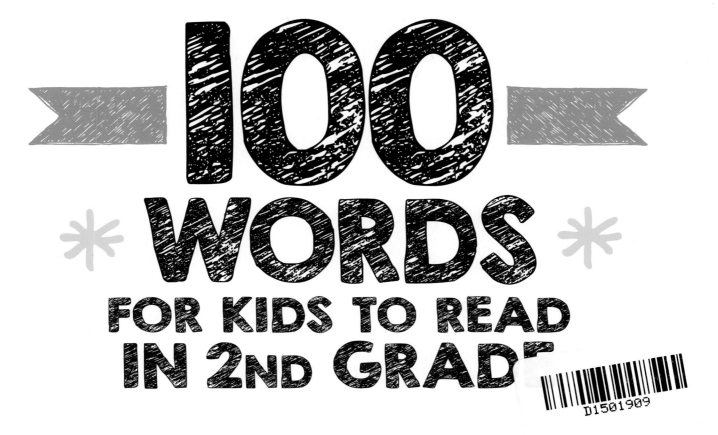

SCHOLASTIC

100 WORDS

FOR KIDS TO READ IN 2ND GRADE

New York • Toronto • London • Auckland • Sydney
Mexico City • New Delhi • Hong Kong • Buenos Aires

Photos ©: cover center left: thawats/iStockphoto; cover center right: pkline/iStockphoto; cover bottom left: m-imagephotography/iStock-photo; cover bottom right: JaysonPhotography/iStockphoto; 3, 4 various stickers: invincible_bulldog/iStockphoto, nata789/iStockphoto, Picnote/iStockphoto; 5: Kang Sunghee/Shutterstock; 6 top: Wavebreakmedia/iStockphoto; 6 center top: HearttoHeart0225/iStockphoto; 6 center bottom: skynesher/iStockphoto; 6 bottom: Steve Debenport/iStockphoto; 7 left: Jeka/Shutterstock; 7 right: SerrNovik/iStock-photo; 8: RusN/iStockphoto; 9: 200mm/iStockphoto; 11 blue paper: Pavel Hlystov/iStockphoto; 11 dog: Ermolaev Alexander/Shutterstock; 12 top: Tyler Olson/Shutterstock; 12 bottom: CarolinaSmith/iStockphoto; 13: Tetyana Kaganska/Shutterstock; 15 top: Rido/Shutterstock; 15 center top: AJP/Shutterstock; 15 center bottom: andresr/iStockphoto; 15 bottom: kali9/iStockphoto; 16: MaxTopchij/iStockphoto; 18: aodaodaod/iStockphoto; 19: Africa Studio/Shutterstock; 20: huePhotography/iStockphoto; 20 right sunflower: matejmm/iStockphoto; 21: RusN/iStockphoto; 24: boitano/iStockphoto; 26: Rouzes/iStockphoto; 27: LightField Studios/Shutterstock; 28: oriental/Shutterstock; 29: bertos/iStockphoto; 32 frame: benz190/iStockphoto; 33: Rawpixel.com/Shutterstock; 34: TheCrimsonMonkey/iStockphoto; 35: Creativa Images/Shutterstock; 36: evemilla/iStockphoto; 37: pic_studio/iStockphoto; 38: Nanette_Grebe/iStockphoto; 40: mustafagull/iStock-photo; 41: Be Good/Shutterstock; 42: karandaev/iStockphoto; 43: Africa Studio/Shutterstock; 44: MediaProduction/iStockphoto; 46: Nirad/iStockphoto; 47: Hogan Imaging/Shutterstock; 48: gmatsuno/iStockphoto; 49: Traimak/Shutterstock; 50: bertos/iStockphoto; 52: Sergei Vakurov/Shutterstock; 53: Savany/iStockphoto; 55: MA8/Shutterstock.

Editor: Ourania Papacharalambous
Cover design: Tannaz Fassihi and Michelle H. Kim
Interior design: Michelle H. Kim

ISBN: 978-1-338-32311-5
Copyright © 2018 by Scholastic Inc.
All rights reserved.
Printed in the U.S.A.
First printing, September 2018.

3 4 5 6 7 8 9 10   40   24 23 22

Dear Parent,

Teachers know and experts agree that the only way for children to master sight words—those high-frequency, often nondecodable words essential to reading fluency—is through practice. With *100 Words for Kids to Read in 2nd Grade*, we are pleased to offer a tool to help your child practice essential sight words in an engaging, effective format.

We created the book with the guidance of literacy experts and classroom teachers. Broken down into manageable groups, words are introduced in context and reinforced through inviting puzzles and games. Each sequence of activities is carefully designed to touch on reading, writing, and usage—taking children beyond mere visual recognition of sight words to genuine mastery. At the end of the book, you'll find a certificate of completion to celebrate your child's accomplishments.

The journey through these skill-building pages will help your child make the successful transition from learning to read to reading to learn. We hope you and your child enjoy the trip!

The Editors

Contents

GROUP 1

answer

could

enough

believe

tell

told

would

knew

know

write

wrote

those

should

these

Scrambled Words

➡ **Unscramble the letters below to make words from the word box.**

answer	those	believe	knew	would
told	tell	could	write	enough

1. r e i w t   _____

2. u c l d o   _____

3. e l l t   _____

4. o l d t   _____

5. n w k e   _____

6. a s n e w r   _____

7. i b e e v e l   _____

8. t h e s o   _____

9. d o w u l   _____

10. o e g n u h   _____

Which Word?

➡️ **Read the story. Then answer each question with a blue word from the story. We did the first one for you.**

"You won't **believe** what I'm going to **tell** you about William."

"I **told** you I don't like to hear gossip."

"Well, if I **wrote** it down then you **could** read it instead of hearing it."

"Even if you **write** it, it's still gossip."

"I **knew** that. Maybe I **should** just keep it to myself."

1. Which blue word is a homophone (a word that sounds the same, but has a different meaning) of the word *new*?

_____knew_____

2. Which blue word is a homophone of the word *right*?

_____

3. Which blue word is the present tense of the verb *told*?

_____

4. Which blue word is the past tense of the verb *write*?

_____

5. Which blue word comes between *apple* and *car* in the dictionary?

_____

6. Which two blue words rhyme?

_____

_____

Clue Starters

 Follow the directions. Then write the circled letters to spell a sight word.

ENOUGH
SHOULD
TELL
THESE
KNEW
BELIEVE

Circle every second letter.

1. ⭐T B R E S L G I H E A V T E

___ ___ ___ ___ ___ ___
      2

2. ⭐Y E Z N E O T U Q G R H

___ ___ ___ ___ ___ ___
      4

Circle every third letter.

3. ⭐E K T I G H H T E J F S Q R E

___ ___ ___ ___ ___
     6   10

4. ⭐J K S L M H P Q O W Z U Q D L V A D

___ ___ ___ ___ ___ ___
     8   3

Circle every fourth letter.

5. ⭐R A B T D S T E W M O L D U I L

___ ___ ___ ___
7   1

6. ⭐G H O K A Q R N K L F E T Z V W

___ ___ ___ ___
   9   5

Copy the letters on the numbered lines to answer the question.

What is the name of America's first National Park?

Y___ ___ ___ ___ ___ ___ ___ ___ ___ ___ National Park
 1   2   3   4   5   6   7   8   9   10

Jack's Shoes

➡ **Use the words from the word box to complete the story.**
Then follow the directions to solve the riddle below.
Remember to capitalize the first word in a sentence.

know	those	would	enough
these	answer	believes	could

Jack ___ ___ ___ ___ ___ like new sneakers.
                      1

___ ___ ___ ___ ___ are his old sneakers.
2

___ ___ ___ ___ ___ are the ones he wants.
    3   **4**

Every time Jack goes up the hill with Jill,

he falls down and breaks his crown. He

___ ___ ___ ___ ___ ___ ___ ___ the problem is his sneakers. Jack told me
              5

if he had a good pair, he ___ ___ ___ ___ ___ get to the top without falling.
                                        6

Are new shoes ___ ___ ___ ___ ___ ___ to help Jack? I don't
              7

___ ___ ___ ___ the ___ ___ ___ ___ ___ ___. It could be that
8   **9**   **10**

Jack is just clumsy!

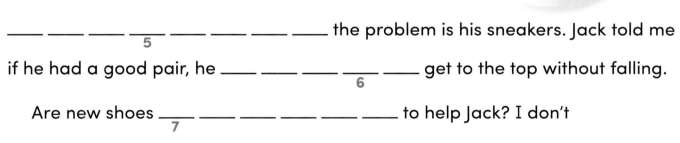

Now try this!
Copy the letters on the numbered lines to solve the riddle below.

What wears shoes but has no feet?

___ ___ ___   ___ ___ ___ ___ ___ ___ ___ ___!
 2 **3** **7**   **4** **5** **1** **7** **10** **9** **6** **8**

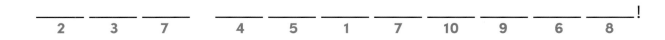

Code Words

Use the decoder to write sight words on the lines below.

1. _____ _____ _____ _____ _____ _____
▶ ◇ ★ ✖ ▮ ●

2. _____ _____ _____ _____ _____
◖ ★ ✖ ⬟ ○

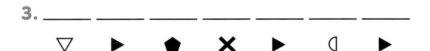

3. _____ _____ _____ _____ _____ _____ _____
▽ ▶ ⬟ ✕ ▶ ◖ ▶

4. _____ _____ _____ _____ _____ _____
▲ ◇ □ ◆ ▶ ⬡

Decoder			
A	▲	N	◇
B	▽	O	★
C	◖	P	♥
D	○	Q	◗
E	▶	R	⬡
F	⬠	S	□
G	▮	T	⬭
H	●	U	✖
I	✕	V	◖
J	■	W	◆
K	△	X	0
L	⬟	Y	◁
M	⬬	Z	⬢

Use each decoded sight word in a sentence.

1. _____

_____

2. _____

_____

3. _____

_____

4. _____

_____

Dogs Can't Spell

➡ **Molly the Mutt has something to tell your teacher, but she can't spell very well. Can you help? Find and circle eight misspelled words in the letter. Then write them correctly on the lines. We did the first one for you.**

Dear Teacher,

The first thing I shood say is that I'm sorry. Sort of.

Let me explain. I no there are times when a student comes to class without his or her homework. You ask where it is, and the student ansers, "The dog ate it!"

"Who wuold beleive such a story?" you say. "Please tell the truth."

Well, I'm righting this letter to tel you it's all true. I, Molly the Mutt, eat homework. Lots of it. I gobble homework everywhere I go.

It all started when I was just a puppy. That's when I tasted my first book report on *Green Eggs and Ham*. Delicious! Now, I'll eat anything I can get my paws on. I like stories, spelling tests, even math workbooks. I can't get enuff!

So, the next time a student shows up with a scrap of paper covered in slobber, think of me.

Yours truly,

Molly the Mutt

1. __should__

2. _____

3. _____

4. _____

5. _____

6. _____

7. _____

8. _____

This Cow Can't Spell

➤ **Use the words from the word box to complete the letter.**

those	would	know	believe	tell	write

Greetings, Earthlings!

We all ___ ___ ___ ___ that the dish ran away

with the spoon, and they lived happily ever after.

I bet you ___ ___ ___ ___ ___ never

___ ___ ___ ___ ___ ___ ___ what happened to me

after my famous jump over the moon. I decided to

___ ___ ___ ___ ___ to ___ ___ ___ ___ you the whole

story. Yes, I jumped over the moon, but I did not land back on

Earth. I kept flying all the way to the planet Venus. Now, I live here.

Life on Venus is a little bit strange. Let me try to explain. On Venus, a day is

longer than a year! I know, I know, it's confusing. And the weather is not great.

Sometimes the temperature rises to 900°F! On ___ ___ ___ ___ ___ days,

I don't go outside. I just stay in and send emails to my herd back on Earth.

So, now you know where I am. I hope you will send me some mail soon.

Now try this!
Put the words from the word box in ABC order.

1. _____

2. _____

3. _____

4. _____

5. _____

6. _____

GROUP 2

bought

drew

hold

buy

brought

thought

laugh

bring

held

talk

hurt

walk

draw

think

Find the Word

➡️ **Complete the sentences below with words from the word box.**
Then find the words in the puzzle. Words may be hidden ➡, ⬇, ↘ or ↗.
We did the first one for you.

1. Have you ___thought___ about what you'd like for your birthday?

2. Hannah likes to _____ home from school.

3. Last Friday, I _____ a new notebook.

4. Today I will _____ the notebook to school with me.

5. Ruthie and Carlos like to _____ pictures of aliens.

6. May I _____ your hand if I get scared during the movie?

7. Sometimes we _____ too loudly in the library.

8. Tanya used colored pencils when she _____ that picture.

B	T	B	R	I	N	G	T
D	H	E	Q	E	Q	H	S
R	O	J	O	D	G	X	K
A	U	O	Q	U	R	L	B
W	G	H	O	E	A	D	P
D	H	B	O	W	M	R	F
P	T	V	K	L	L	E	M
T	A	L	K	S	D	W	F

bought
bring
~~thought~~
hold
drew
draw
walk
talk

Scrambled Words

Unscramble the letters below to make words from the word box.

bring	buy	drew	hold	laugh
think	walk	bought	brought	draw

1. k w l a _____

2. l o h d _____

3. g a u h l _____

4. g o h t b r u _____

5. a w r d _____

6. b y u _____

7. d w r e _____

8. n r i g b _____

9. t i h k n _____

10. b g h o u t _____

Match It!

➡️ **A synonym is a word that means the same or almost the same as another word. Read the story. Then find the synonym for each blue word from the word box. We did the first one for you.**

Justin **took** his pet pig, Hoggy, to school. He **cradled** Hoggy in his lap during class. Every time Ms. Lawrence started to **speak**, Hoggy started to oink! Ms. Lawrence didn't **suppose** it was such a good idea to have a pig at school. So Denise asked if she could **purchase** a rooster for the classroom instead. We all started to **giggle**. Ms. Lawrence laughed so hard her stomach **ached**!

1. took   <u>brought</u>

2. cradled   _____

3. speak   _____

4. suppose   _____

5. purchase   _____

6. giggle   _____

7. ached   _____

think

laugh

talk

~~brought~~

held

buy

hurt

A-maze-ing Verbs

➡️ **To complete the maze, pass only through the correct sentences.
An incorrect sentence is like a wall in the maze: You cannot pass through it.
The correct path takes you through nine circles.**

START

Lilly **drew** a picture.

Lilly **draw** a picture.

Jake and Sam **writes** stories.

I **talks** a lot.

Sam **held** his nose.

Jake and Sam **buys** candy.

Lilly **brought** Pete to school.

Jake **thought** hard.

Sam **wrote** a letter.

Lilly **thinked** Sam was nice.

Jake **bought** some candy.

Yesterday, Lilly **bring** Pete to school.

Jake **laughed** at Sam's joke.

Lilly and Pete **walked** home.

Sam **hurted** his toe.

FINISH

My head **hurts**.

Sports Puzzle

➡ **Use the words from the word box to complete the sentences below. Then write the words in the correct spaces in the puzzle. We did the first one for you.**

hold	think	bring	laugh
~~bought~~	walk	thought	drew

Across

3. I _____bought_____ myself a new baseball mitt with my allowance money.

5. Did you _____ your consent form for the away game?

6. What do you _____ about the new stadium? I like it a lot.

8. My mother drives me to softball practice in the morning, but I _____ home in the afternoon.

Down

1. We always _____ at the mascot's jokes.

2. I _____ Jim would love tennis, but he prefers soccer.

4. Marcus likes to draw. He _____ a picture of his teammates.

7. "Free divers" swim without a snorkel or scuba gear; they _____ their breath under water.

GROUP 3

because

around

behind

above

does

below

done

far

flew

fly

through

grow

very

grew

going

Scrambled Words

➡️ Unscramble the letters below to make words from the word box.

because	done	grew	through	very
above	behind	below	far	grow

1. o d e n   _____

2. w g o r   _____

3. b w o e l   _____

4. r v e y   _____

5. h u g t o r h   _____

6. s a u c e e b   _____

7. b e a v o   _____

8. d b n i e h   _____

9. g w r e   _____

10. a f r   _____

Clue Starters

➡ **Follow the directions. Then write the circled letters to spell a sight word.**

Circle every second letter.

1. ⭐T A Q R M O C U B N R D

  ___ ___ ___ ___ ___
      8   3   4

2. ⭐T B P E J H L I M N F D

  ___ ___ ___ ___ ___
      7   1

Circle every third letter.

3. ⭐G P D N I O E Z E O P S

  ___ ___ ___ ___
          2

4. ⭐E Z G L J R I T E M N W

  ___ ___ ___
     6

Circle every fourth letter.

5. ⭐W Z Q F N P R A P S O R

  ___ ___ ___
      5

6. ⭐N I R F U L P L B C A Y

  ___ ___ ___

BEHIND
FAR
DOES
FLY
AROUND
GREW

Copy the letters on the numbered lines to answer the question.

What is the longest body of water in the U.S.?

M ___ ___ ___ ___ ___ ___   ___ ___ V ___ ___
   1   2   2   3   4   5   1   6   1   7   8

A-maze-ing Birds

➡️ **To complete the maze, pass only through the correct sentences. An incorrect sentence is like a wall in the maze. The right path goes through seven circles.**

When they were done, she got more food.

She feeds her babies worms so they grows.

When they was done, she got more food.

She fed her babies so they would grow.

A mother bird does a lot of work!

A mother bird do a lot of work!

A mother bird fly with a worm.

I began going to see them every day.

START

I saw her flew into her nest.

A bird flew with a worm in her mouth.

I saw her fly into her nest.

The mother bird done a lot of work!

She fed her babies so they growed.

I goed to see the birds every day.

The babies growed and flew away.

The babies grew and flew away.

FINISH

The babies flew and flyed away.

Code Words

➡ **Use the decoder to write sight words on the lines below.**

1. _____ _____ _____ _____ _____ _____ _____

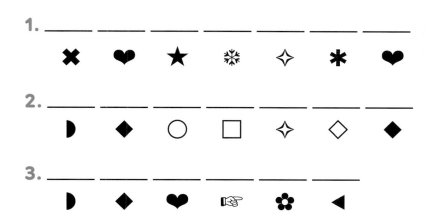

2. _____ _____ _____ _____ _____ _____ _____

3. _____ _____ _____ _____ _____ _____

4. _____ _____ _____ _____ _____ _____

Decoder			
A	□	N	✿
B	◐	O	❄
C	○	P	▮
D	◀	Q	△
E	◆	R	★
F	▽	S	◇
G	✳	T	✖
H	♥	U	✧
I	☞	V	●
J	■	W	▼
K	☆	X	➤
L	▲	Y	♡
M	✔	Z	▢

Use each decoded sight word in a sentence.

1. _____

_____

2. _____

_____

3. _____

_____

4. _____

_____

Herman the Class Dragon

➡️ **Use the words from the word box to complete the story below.**

around	behind	because	done	does
flew	grew	going	through	above

Our teacher returned from vacation with a very small

dragon. We named him Herman _____

when we said, "Herman," he flared his nostrils and looked

like he was _____ to smile. We kept him in

a big tank. That way, we could look _____

the glass and watch him sleep or reach his head

_____ his body to lick his wings clean.

As Herman got bigger, his wings also

_____. One of our class jobs was lifting

Herman high _____ our heads so that he could practice flapping

his wings. We would have one kid supporting him from the front and another

_____ him. Afterward, we would pet Herman's scales and tell him

he had _____ a good job. Practicing seemed to tire him out.

That is until last Monday, when Herman _____ up and

perched on top of the highest bookshelf. He gave us a toothy smile, the way

he sometimes _____, and flapped his wings proudly.

Sort It Out!

➡ **Put each word from the word box in the circle where it belongs. We did the first one for you.**

~~above~~	does	flew
behind	far	around
below	fly	grow
going		

Action Words

_____

_____

_____

_____

_____

Words that Answer *Where?*

above

_____

_____

_____

_____

Now try this!

Write a sentence using as many words from the word box as you can.

_____

_____

How many words from the word box did you use? _____

Pedal Puzzle

➡ **Use the words from the word box to complete the sentences below. Then write the words in the correct spaces in the puzzle. We did the first one for you.**

above	below	around
behind	far	through
because	very	

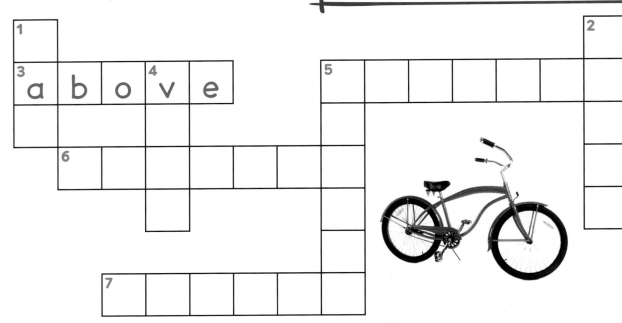

Across

3. When I ride my bike, the street is under my tires, and the sky is _____above_____ my head.

5. I have to put air in my tires _____ they are flat.

6. When you pump up your tires, make sure the air is coming _____ the hose.

7. We like to ride our bikes _____ our neighborhood.

Down

1. The distance from my house to my friend's isn't _____.

2. As I pedal, I can see the ground move _____ my feet.

4. Our neighborhood is a _____ interesting place to explore.

5. I ride in front and my friend rides _____ me.

GROUP 4

always

it's

start

wrong

once

just

never

its

left

month

light

right

may

must

year

Which Word?

➡️ **Read the story. Then answer each question with a blue word from the story. We did the first one for you.**

Alisha **always** gets new sneakers at the **start** of the school **year**.

Today, Alisha picks up a blue and white striped sneaker. **It's** perfect. She asks, "**May** I try this on?"

A man checks the size of her **right** foot and then her **left**. Then he brings her the shoes. But when she puts them on, her feet hurt. "These don't fit," she says. That's when she sees that they are on the **wrong** feet!

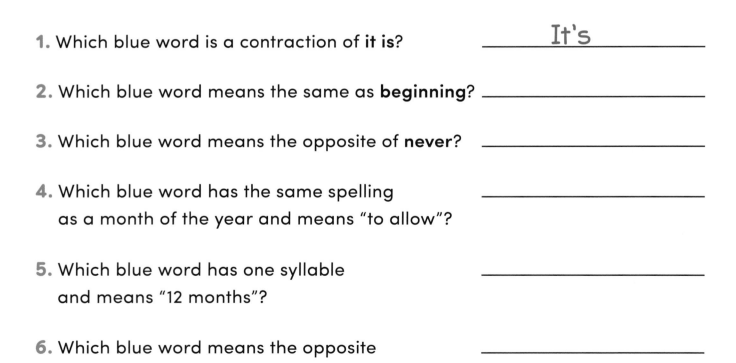

1. Which blue word is a contraction of **it is**? _____It's_____

2. Which blue word means the same as **beginning**? _____

3. Which blue word means the opposite of **never**? _____

4. Which blue word has the same spelling as a month of the year and means "to allow"? _____

5. Which blue word has one syllable and means "12 months"? _____

6. Which blue word means the opposite of both **left** and **wrong**? _____

My Blue Monster

➡️ **Use the words from the word box to complete the story. Then solve the riddle at the bottom of the page. We did the first one for you.**

always	just	light	month
must	never	~~once~~	

I have a blue monster in my closet. About

o n c e   a ___ ___ ___ ___ ___ ,
   1   2

I move all the coats and shoes and go in

for a visit.

He's ___ ___ ___ ___ ___ ___ a little

cranky at first. "It's bad enough," he growls,

"that you almost ___ ___ ___ ___ ___ come
                    3   4

to see me, but when you do, ___ ___ ___ ___
                                        5

you let in all that ___ ___ ___ ___ ___?" But
                      6

when we play a game, he cheers right up.

Then I say goodbye for another month or so. He ___ ___ ___ ___
                                                    7

growls and says, "Make sure you leave it good and dark when you go."

But I know he'll miss me.

Now try this!

Copy the letters on the numbered lines to solve the riddle.

What do you do with a blue monster?

___ ___ ___ ___ ___   ___ ___   ___ p!
 1   2   3   3   4   6   5   7

Mystery Letter

➡ **In each set of words, the same letter is missing. Can you find the mystery letter in each set? The letters you need are in the Letter Box.**

Letter Box

t e h r b a

1. ____elow

____ecause

____ehind

The mystery letter is _____.

2. yea____

sta____t

w____ong

The mystery letter is _____.

3. onc____

n____ver

l____ft

The mystery letter is _____.

4. ____lways

m____y

w____lk

The mystery letter is _____.

5. i____s

jus____

mus____

The mystery letter is _____.

6. lig____t

rig____t

mont____

The mystery letter is _____.

Now try this!

To answer the riddle, fill in the six mystery letters in the order they appear.

What can you hold without using your hands?

Your ____ ____ ____ ____ ____ ____!
     1   2   3   4   5   6

Code Words

➡ **Use the decoder to write sight words on the lines below.**

Decoder			
A	○	N	✖
B	◊	O	⬡
C	■	P	□
D	★	Q	◗
E	▲	R	✿
F	▽	S	▷
G	◖	T	▮
H	◆	U	●
I	▶	V	◖
J	⬠	W	◇
K	△	X	⬣
L	⬟	Y	♥
M	⬮	Z	◗

1. _____ _____ _____

2. _____ _____ _____
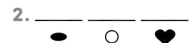

3. _____ _____ _____ _____
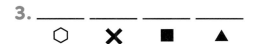

4. _____ _____ _____ _____

Use each decoded sight word in a sentence.

1. _____

_____

2. _____

_____

3. _____

_____

4. _____

_____

Word Search

Find the words in the puzzle below. Words are hidden →, ↓, ↘ and ↗.

ALWAYS	JUST	LEFT	LIGHT	MONTH
MUST	NEVER	RIGHT	WRONG	YEAR

```
N Y N Q T R N H K F L
L J W E D K J F Q J E
R I A X V P F E L H F
Q I G P I E G M U S T
H Q G H W N R D I Y S
J O Z H T V D S M Z X
J C A E T S Y E A R G
U Z Q Y K A W T N Z Y
S F J I W R O N G Y N
T L G L Z B D E U D G
C C A R H R Q W R B T
B F M Z Y M O N T H V
```

GROUP 5

away

call

full

find

too

shall

pull

only

kind

put

upon

much

found

round

Find the Word

➡️ **Complete the sentences below with words from the word box.
Then find the words in the puzzle. Words may be hidden ➡, ↓, ↘ or ↗.
We did the first one for you.**

1. I chose a pumpkin that had no bumps and was perfectly ___round___.

2. Sarah had a question about her homework, so she picked up

the phone to _____ Tanisha.

3. After Juan ate the hot fudge sundae, his stomach felt very

_____.

4. When my mom went _____ on a trip, she
sent me postcards.

5. Success depends _____ how hard you work.

6. Sam had to _____ on his dog's leash to keep
him away from the other dog.

A	R	H	L	U	I
D	W	L	U	P	P
I	A	A	D	O	U
C	E	F	Y	N	L
R	O	U	N	D	L
P	U	F	U	L	L

away
pull
call
round
full
upon

Scrambled Words

Unscramble the letters below to make words from the word box.

find	much	pull	round	upon
too	shall	away	call	found

1. oto _____

2. lupl _____

3. ounp _____

4. ndouf _____

5. mhuc _____

6. dnfi _____

7. lacl _____

8. llhas _____

9. waya _____

10. rnodu _____

Lost and Found

➡ **Read the story. Then fill in the bubble next to the best answer to each question below.**

One day, Alisha's little brother **found** three dollars. "Look!" he said. "Now I can buy a pony!"

"I think a pony will cost too **much**," Alisha said. "**Shall** I help you **find** something to spend it on?"

"Okay," he said. He **put** the money in his pocket.

"Ice cream might be a good thing to spend it on," said Alisha. "What **kind** do you want?"

"I **only** like one kind. Chocolate," said her brother.

"I think chocolate is the best kind, **too**," said Alisha.

1. When Alisha says a pony will cost too **much**, she means:
   - ○ Three dollars is more than enough money to buy a pony.
   - ○ A pony costs a lot more than three dollars.
   - ○ If her brother had found five dollars, he could buy a pony.

2. When Alisha says,"I think chocolate is the best kind, **too**," the word **too** means
   - ○ also.
   - ○ two.
   - ○ not at all.

3. The opposite of **found** is
   - ○ kept.
   - ○ forgot.
   - ○ lost.

4. Which word means the same as **kind** in this story?
   - ○ nice
   - ○ child
   - ○ type

5. In the dictionary, the word **only** appears
   - ○ between *lonely* and *quiet*.
   - ○ after the word *totally*.
   - ○ before the word *night*.

Clue Starters

 Follow the directions. Then write the circled letters to spell a sight word.

Circle every second letter.

1. R   R   T   O   G   U   S   N   H   D

___ ___ ___ ___ ___

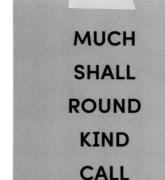

MUCH

SHALL

ROUND

KIND

CALL

FIND

2. Z   S   Y   H   E   A   Q   L   T   L

___ ___ ___ ___ ___
      1   2

Circle every third letter.

3. A   W   M   L   D   U   N   R   C   M   T   H

___ ___ ___ ___

4. G   S   K   I   H   I   M   R   N   S   P   D

___ ___ ___ ___
         3

Circle every fourth letter.

5. D   A   K   C   L   P   N   A   O   N   P   L   Q   Y   S   L

___ ___ ___ ___
  4   5

6. D   N   L   F   A   N   I   I   I   A   G   N   A   P   E   D

___ ___ ___ ___

Copy the letters on the numbered lines to answer the question.

What is the national bird of the United States?

AMERICAN   B ___ ___ ___   E ___ G ___ E
            1   2   3   4   5

Sort It Out!

➡️ **Put each word from the word box in the circle where it belongs. We did the first one for you.**

found	call	round	full
find	put	pull	

Verbs
(action words)

found

_____

_____

_____

_____

Adjectives
(describing words)

_____

_____

_____

_____

Now try this!
Write a sentence using as many words from the word box as you can.

_____

_____

How many words from the word box did you use? _____

Code Words

Use the decoder to write sight words on the lines below.

1. ___ ___ ___ ___
   14 21 14 13

2. ___ ___ ___ ___
   23 12 22 4

3. ___ ___ ___ ___ ___
   3 11 5 22 4

4. ___ ___ ___ ___ ___
   8 11 5 22 4

Decoder			
A	14	N	22
B	26	O	11
C	15	P	10
D	4	Q	24
E	17	R	8
F	3	S	16
G	19	T	25
H	6	U	5
I	12	V	18
J	9	W	21
K	23	X	2
L	1	Y	13
M	7	Z	20

Use each decoded sight word in a sentence.

1. _____

_____

2. _____

_____

3. _____

_____

4. _____

_____

The Missing Rabbit

➤ **Use the words from the word box to complete the letter.**

kind	found	put	away
only	full	call	

Dear Mrs. Washington:

I was given permission to take care of our class rabbit Binky over the summer. Everything was going so well. Then a few weeks ago he disappeared. I _____ "missing bunny" posters everywhere! Then things started getting strange.

First I _____ a copy of the book *The Runaway Bunny* hidden in his cage. Then I got a _____ from the cashier at the supermarket. He said he saw a group of rabbits hopping _____ from the store with bags _____ of stolen goods. Their leader looked like Binky.

At first I didn't believe it. Neither did my friends. But Mrs. Washington I think we both know that the _____ rabbit in this part of the country that is completely white is Binky.

I hope you don't blame me for Binky's actions. I don't know what happened—he was always so _____! Anyway I think our next class pet should be a goldfish.

Sincerely,

Joseph Spelling

GROUP 6

again

live

carry

clean

city

middle

about

own

warm

sure

ready

which

word

though

Puzzle It Out!

➡ **Use the words from the word box to complete the sentences below. Then write the words in the correct spaces in the puzzle.**

Across

1. My name was the first _____ that I learned to spell.

3. Sam washed the dishes so they were sparkling _____.

4. The weather today is _____ but not hot.

5. At the end of second grade, our teacher said we were _____ for third.

Down

2. Will you share my popcorn, or do you want your _____?

3. She has to _____ the baby because he's too little to walk.

6. We had burgers for dinner last night, and we're having them _____ tonight.

clean
again
ready
warm
own
carry
word

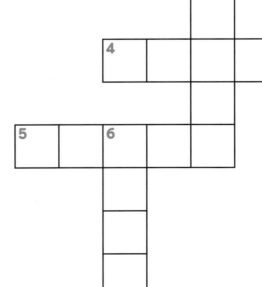

Loony Lunch Time

➡️ **Don't read this story yet! First, write a word on each line in the box on the right. Then put the words in the story and read it out loud.**

Lunch time at _____
1

Elementary sure can get _____.
2

When the bell rings in the **middle** of the day,

kids start _____ toward the
3

cafeteria. But I have to say, the food is usually

_____.
4

I'm not sure **which** dish they serve most often.

It's probably fried _____ or
5

macaroni and _____.
6

I should warn you **though**, there

is a rumor going around **about** the

_____ soup. People say it
7

was made in 19 _____. How
8

_____!
9

Next time you're in the **city** where I **live**,

come on by, and I'll treat you to lunch!

1. _____
   famous person

2. _____
   adjective

3. _____
   verb ending in -ing

4. _____
   adjective

5. _____
   noun

6. _____
   noun (plural)

7. _____
   animal

8. _____
   two-digit number

9. _____
   adjective

Bella's Big Day

➡️ **A synonym is a word that has the same meaning as another word. Read the story. Then find the synonym for each blue word from the word box. We did the first one for you.**

about	carried	clean	~~lives~~
middle	owns	ready	sure

My pet rabbit, Bella, **dwells** in a cage in my backyard. I keep her cage **spotless**. I feed her and pet her. When my teacher said anyone who **possesses** a pet could bring it in for Class Pet Day, I was **prepared**! I **toted** Bella's cage all the way to school on a city bus. It took **around** an hour, but it was

worth it. I put Bella in the **center** of the room, and everyone took turns petting her. I'm **certain** that Bella was the world's happiest rabbit that day.

1. **dwells** _____lives_____

2. **spotless** _____

3. **possesses** _____

4. **prepared** _____

5. **toted** _____

6. **around** _____

7. **center** _____

8. **certain** _____

Code Words

 Use the decoder to write sight words on the lines below.

1. ___ ___ ___ ___ ___
2. ___ ___ ___ ___ ___
3. ___ ___ ___ ___ ___
4. ___ ___ ___ ___ ___

	Decoder		
A	❖	N	■
B	◉	O	▽
C	❯	P	☆
D	❄	Q	❶
E	❧	R	❑
F	→	S	▲
G	▯	T	▼
H	✳	U	◆
I	▶	V	➤
J	❋	W	◗
K	✚	X	△
L	●	Y	♠
M	○	Z	▮

Use each decoded sight word in a sentence.

1. _____

_____

2. _____

_____

3. _____

_____

4. _____

_____

Word Search

Find the words in the puzzle below. Words are hidden →, ↓, ↘ and ↗.

AGAIN	CITY	LIVE	MIDDLE	READY
SURE	THOUGH	WARM	WHICH	WORD

```
W  P  L  I  V  E  Z  I  Z  N  M  A
A  I  E  S  N  Y  K  R  W  Q  S  T
R  M  M  Z  T  B  T  J  E  O  A  V
M  I  K  I  N  X  H  M  R  B  R  I
G  D  C  D  Y  C  O  W  F  D  L  D
E  D  Q  V  I  O  Z  X  H  B  E  J
S  L  Y  H  C  P  M  G  I  C  C  W
U  E  W  G  N  U  U  R  Y  A  Y  Q
R  Y  J  Q  N  O  A  L  T  D  K  A
E  U  E  V  H  G  H  Q  A  N  S  L
K  I  R  T  G  X  N  E  X  H  U  M
A  G  A  I  N  Y  R  T  I  U  W  T
```

46

© Scholastic Inc.

GROUP 7

beautiful

different

tomorrow

neither

frighten

yesterday

straight

today

either

together

several

learn

trouble

been

A Winning Story

Use the words from the word box to complete the story below. We did the first one for you. Remember to capitalize the first word in a sentence.

either	several	today
neither	been	tomorrow
~~together~~	yesterday	different

Carlos and Anna play

checkers **together** almost

every day. They play again and again.

_____ one likes to lose.

Carlos has _____ the

winner _____ times.

When they played _____, Anna won every game.

_____, _____ one could win. Maybe they

should play a _____ game _____!

Now try this!

Put the words from the word box in ABC order.
We did the first one for you.

1. **been**

2. _____

3. _____

4. _____

5. _____

6. _____

7. _____

8. _____

9. _____

48

© Scholastic Inc.

Scrambled Words

➡️ **Unscramble the letters below to make words from the word box.**

been	different	today	together	either
neither	yesterday	trouble	frighten	beautiful

1. h i n e r e t _____

2. b u t l o e r _____

3. n e b e _____

4. g h t n e f i r _____

5. d e a s y e y t r _____

6. e t l u i a u b f _____

7. e d i n f t f e r _____

8. t o a y d _____

9. h r t e t g o e _____

10. h r i e t e _____

A Monstrous Maze

➡️ **Read this ad for Fright Boosters Night School. Then complete the maze by passing only through the true sentences. The correct path takes you through seven boxes.**

Attention, Monsters! Do you have **trouble** scaring humans? Has a little old lady ever told you you're **beautiful**? Do you sometimes worry that you couldn't **frighten** a small child?

Don't worry. Being scary is a skill you can **learn**. And at Fright Boosters Night School, we can teach you. Soon, little old ladies will faint at the sight of you. Grown men will leap **straight** into the air at your growl. Call today!

START

Another word for **trouble** is **difficulty**.

The opposite of **beautiful** is **ugly**.

Another word for **beautiful** is **ugly**.

The opposite of **beautiful** is **pretty**.

Another word for **beautiful** is **pretty**.

Frighten means the same as **scare**.

The opposite of **frighten** is **scare**.

Another word for **frighten** is **laugh**.

Another word for **learn** is **forget**.

To **learn**, one must **study** or **practice**.

Another word for **learn** is **teach**.

In this story, **straight** means **crooked**.

In this story, **straight** means **directly**.

Straight rhymes with **eight**.

Straight has an **f** sound, like **enough**.

FINISH

50

Clue Starters

➡ **Follow the directions. Then write the circled letters to spell a sight word.**

Circle every second letter.

1. Q S R E J V X E H R Y A M L

___ ___ ___ ___ ___ ___ ___ ___
  13   5

2. R Y T E P S V T N E O R L D M A Q Y

___ ___ ___ ___ ___ ___ ___ ___ ___
        3   10   2

Circle every third letter.

3. K N T M O O T U M P Z O L S R R W R Q I O W O W

___ ___ ___ ___ ___ ___ ___ ___
    8

4. N J S M T T O R R D L A M T I W B G E B H I S T

___ ___ ___ ___ ___ ___ ___ ___
      12   4

Circle every fourth letter.

5. N I D L M S R E O Y Z A M N B R L R L N

___ ___ ___ ___ ___
    7   1

6. K L O E M N O I B A F T K N V H R Q W E N Z H R

___ ___ ___ ___ ___ ___
 9   11   6

Copy the letters on the numbered lines to answer the question.

Who were the first people to live in America?

___ ___ ___ ___ ___ ___
 1   2   3   4   5   6

___ ___ ___ ___ ___ C ___ ___ ___
7   8   9 10 11   12 1 13

Aliens Can't Spell

The alien who wrote this ad can't spell very well! Can you help? Find and circle nine misspelled words. Then write the words correctly on the lines below.

If you're from the planet Gooeygoopiter, listen up! Do you have trubble with slime? Has it bin oozing from your ears and toes? When you get togehter with human friends, do your feet leave embarrassing gooey marks on their carpets?

What you are about to lern will change all of that. SLIME AWAY is the first slime remover made for stubborn problems like yours.

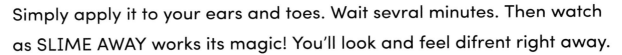

Simply apply it to your ears and toes. Wait sevral minutes. Then watch as SLIME AWAY works its magic! You'll look and feel difrent right away.

Behind all that slime, there's a beautifull alien! So why wait until tomorow when you can be slime-less twoday?

1. _____ 4. _____ 7. _____

2. _____ 5. _____ 8. _____

3. _____ 6. _____ 9. _____

Word Search

Find the words in the puzzle below. Words are hidden →, ↓, ↘ and ↗.

BEAUTIFUL	DIFFERENT	EITHER	FRIGHTEN
LEARN	NEITHER	SEVERAL	STRAIGHT
TODAY	TOGETHER	TOMORROW	TROUBLE

```
O  T  R  O  U  B  L  E  D  K  G  O
S  X  P  O  T  O  M  O  R  R  O  W
K  Y  D  I  F  F  E  R  E  N  T  Q
P  E  C  X  Y  W  A  T  R  N  L  H
S  E  V  E  R  A  L  E  E  U  E  O
S  T  R  A  I  G  H  T  F  Z  I  N
W  M  L  H  U  T  H  I  O  Y  T  E
M  S  W  E  E  G  T  L  P  O  H  I
Q  V  F  G  I  U  O  O  D  B  E  T
W  V  O  R  A  Y  I  A  D  A  R  H
N  T  F  E  M  E  Y  N  T  A  K  E
P  R  B  G  A  L  E  A  R  N  Y  R
```

My 100 Words

Group 1

answer	know	told
believe	should	would
could	tell	write
enough	these	wrote
knew	those	

Group 2

bought	drew	talk
bring	held	think
brought	hold	thought
buy	hurt	walk
draw	laugh	

Group 3

above	does	going
around	done	grew
because	far	grow
behind	flew	through
below	fly	very

Group 4

always	light	once
it's	may	right
its	month	start
just	must	wrong
left	never	year

Group 5

away	kind	round
call	much	shall
find	only	too
found	pull	upon
full	put	

Group 6

about	live	though
again	middle	warm
carry	own	which
city	ready	word
clean	sure	

Group 7

beautiful	been	different	frighten	either	learn	neither
several	straight	today	together	tomorrow	trouble	yesterday

NAME THAT
WORD!

Name That Word!

through

Name That Word!

neither

shall

Name That Word!

because

Name That Word!

Name That Word!

straight

Name That Word! Board Game

(See page 58 for directions on how to play.)

Start

bring

Pick a card.

Spell a word that sounds the same as *witch* but is a question word.

call

Go ahead one space.

clean

Say a word that rhymes with *sink* and means "what you do with your mind."

Pick a card.

Say a word that is the past tense of the verb *buy*.

could

Pick a card.

Say a word that means the same as *too.*

Say a word that means the same as *middle.*

far

Go back one space.

wrote

draw

Pick a card.

Spell a word that sounds the same as *write* but means "the opposite of wrong."

flew

Pick a card.

Say the word that means "the day before today."

those

Go ahead one space.

Say a word that means the same as *frighten*.

kind

Say a word that means the opposite of *laugh*.

Say a word that means the opposite of *above*.

knew

may

Go back one space.

Pick a card.

Say the word that means the same as "12 months."

fly

Pick a card.

Say a word that means the same as *done*.

Say the word that is the past tense of the verb *hurt*.

Pick a card.

much

Say a word that rhymes with *show* and means "to get bigger."

hold

Pick a card.

Say a word that means the same as *below*.

talk

Pick a card.

Spell a word that sounds the same as *no* but means "to understand."

light

end

Say a word that means the opposite of *full*.

Say a word that means the opposite of *found*.

Finish

Name That Word!

BOARD GAME

What You Need to Play

- The game board on pages 56–57

- Word Cards (cut from pages 59–62)

- Two players

- A game piece, such as a coin or a button, for each player

- One die

How to Play

- Place all the Word Cards facedown in a pile.

- Roll the die. Move your piece the number of dots on the die.

- If you land on a pink circle, say a word that rhymes with the word in the circle.

- If you land on "Pick a Card," your partner picks a Word Card and reads the word on the card out loud. You have to spell it. If you spell the word correctly, move ahead one space. After you follow the directions on that space, it is your partner's turn.

- If you land on any other circle, follow the directions.

- The first person to reach *Finish* wins!

again	answer	beautiful
because	been	behind
brought	city	does
live	neither	once

Name
That
Word!

Name
That
Word!

Name
That
Word!

Name
That
Word!

Name
That
Word!

Name
That
Word!

Name
That
Word!

Name
That
Word!

Name
That
Word!

Name
That
Word!

Name
That
Word!

Name
That
Word!

pull	several	shall
start	straight	tell
thought	through	tomorrow
trouble	warm	word

Name That Word!

Name That Word!

Name That Word!

Name That Word!

Name That Word!

Name That Word!

Name That Word!

Name That Word!

Name That Word!

Name That Word!

Name That Word!

Name That Word!

FOR OUTSTANDING ACHIEVEMENT

CONGRATULATIONS!

This certificate is awarded to

I'm proud of you!